LANDSCAPE

LOOKING AT Art

Chris Dunn

Hodder & Stoughton
A MEMBER OF THE HODDER HEADLINE GROUP

Introduction: landscapes

Netherlandish Painting, artist unknown, **Landscape: A River among Mountains,** c. 16th century, oil on wood, 50.8 × 68.6 cm (19⅞ × 26⅞ inches), The National Gallery, London.

Images of landscapes can be created to describe what a place is like, rather like a postcard.

They can create a mood, like a gathering storm or a hot summer's day.

They can make you feel good or scared or overawed.

They can be created from the imagination.

They can show you dramatic places made even more wonderful by the work of the artist or craftsperson. Often the real image of the landscape is changed by the artist's vision.

Images of landscapes have always been a popular theme in art. They can give you historical information. Through the images you can see different cultures and different artists' styles.

Look carefully at the Netherlandish painting. In the corner under the tall tree sits the artist recording the clear, almost dreamlike detail of this early landscape. It is one of the earliest examples of a landscape painted on its own, rather than as a background for the main subject of the picture.

Activity

*Find other early paintings with landscapes depicted in the background. Can you find some examples of other early paintings which are **only** of landscapes?*

Mark Copeland (b.1956), **The Rising Sun**, 1991, oil on canvas, 86.4 × 114.3 cm (34 × 45 inches), Portal Gallery, London.

Writing a statement of intent: target setting

Try to develop the habit of setting targets as you start each new project. Then, when the work is finished, you can measure your achievement.

Here are some ways of doing this.

- What's it all about?
- Decide on the content or storyline of your work. Write it down.
- How are you going to do it?
- Think about the way your work will be presented.
- What materials will you use?
- What research do you need to do?

Now write down exactly what you are going to do. Your ideas may change as the work progresses but you should be able to develop your statement as your ideas evolve. You should have a clear written statement to measure your progress against.

Look at Mark Copeland's painting.

The figure has taken over the landscape. She is clothed in the rich greens of the forest and the patterns of grazing and ploughland. She is the Earth Mother that ancient religions believed gave fertility to the land. With one finger she stirs the river while in the early morning village, breakfasts are being cooked on newly stoked fires. This is the way an artist has imagined the landscape.

Activity

Collect information for landscape work by going out with a sketchbook, a camera and a collecting bag and undertake your work in a real landscape environment. Aim to create a piece of work that grows as you get more experience. Write a statement of intent so that you and your teacher can review your progress against it.

Discussion point

★ How might this artist imagine a desert or an ice sheet landscape?

What are landscapes for?

John Constable (1776–1837), **The White Horse**, 1819, oil on canvas, 131 × 188 cm (51 × 73 5/16 inches), © The Frick Collection, New York. Many drawings, cloud studies and a lifetime's knowledge of his subject preceded this oil sketch.

John Constable thought the best way to discover a landscape was to explore it by foot. In his painting *The White Horse* he shows how knowledge gained by living, walking and sketching in the landscape can be put to good use. His painting on this page shows a very clear view of this part of the river. He described the place he was painting as 'on the river between Dedham in Suffolk at a point where a tributary interrupted the towpath'. He must have seen the horses being ferried across dozens of times. The place can still be visited and recognised today.

Activity

Set your targets!

An artist uses skill to describe a landscape. Find a landscape you would like to share with others. Use your research skills to find out all you can about it. Make a photographic or drawn record from life. Collect all your research in your sketchbook.

When you feel you know your subject really well create a finished piece. Use the information on target setting on page 3 to help you achieve this.

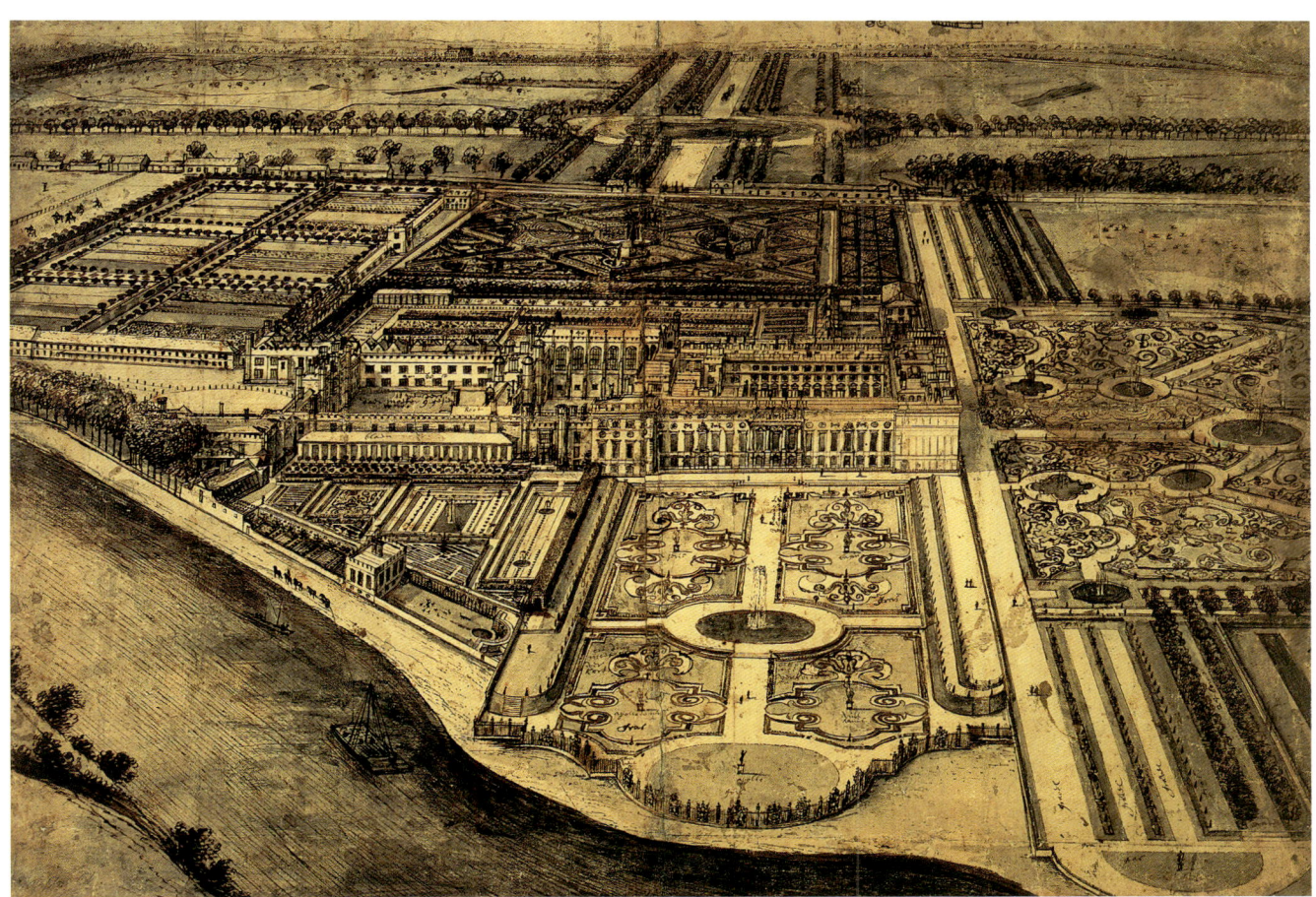

Leonard Kynff (1650–1722),
Hampton Court from the South, 1702,
pen and brown ink with a grey wash,
41.3 × 58.5 cm (16 1/16 × 22 13/16 inches),
The British Museum, London.

This drawing by Leonard Kynff is an accountant's drawing. It was produced to show King William III how his new palace of Hampton Court would look when it was finished. The artist has invented this aerial perspective. As a description it had to be accurate — William would have used it to keep track of construction work as the Palace was being built.

Evaluation

Can you redraw your landscape from a different angle? Use only your first piece of work. Can you draw a ground plan or map of your landscape using your original research?

The ease and accuracy with which you complete this task is a measure of the quality of your research.

Extension

Create a landscape that, like Kynff's, looks into the future. For example, it could be an airport, caravan park, or leisure park.

You might find it useful to base your work on an existing photograph or an illustration of real, undeveloped countryside.

Using a sketchbook: John Constable

John Constable (1776–1837), **Stonehenge**, 1820, pencil sketch made on the site, 11.5 × 18.7 cm (4½ × 7⅜ inches), Victoria & Albert Museum, London.

Look at how Constable has used his sketches to develop his final painting.

Through your landscape studies try and develop a methodical use of your sketchbook.

A sketch is a careful drawing that helps you to understand your subject. It also helps you to plan ahead.

A sketch is carried out to give information.

Sometimes written notes are an important part of a sketch. You might use colour over one part of a sketch.

Often you can't return to a site, so it is important to get as much information as you can in as few visits as possible.

John Constable (1776–1837), **Stonehenge**, 1836, pencil sketch squared up to enlarge and transfer, 15.1 × 26.6 cm (5⅞ × 9¹⁵/₁₆ inches), Courtauld Institute of Art, University of London, London.

Activity

Make some drawings of a landscape. It need not be as dramatic as Stonehenge, but look for detail or interesting shapes. Those forgotten, untidy bits of garden or field corners make good subjects for study.

When you have discovered your landscape make a full study of it in your sketchbook.

Make sure your record is complete as you may not be able to return to the site.

John Constable (1776–1837), **Stonehenge**, 1836, watercolour, 15.4 × 25.3 cm (6 × 10 inches), Victoria & Albert Museum, London.

How sketches may be used

If you want to make a study of a descriptive landscape, you will need factual information, even measured details. It will help if you write down your intentions before you sketch. It could also help focus your mind.

Above all develop your curiosity and collect as many different sketches as possible. These may supply the solutions to the unresolved problems that fill every good artist's sketchbooks.

In the watercolour picture of Stonehenge, Constable tries to capture the mystery of the place. In 1836, when this was painted, little was known about its history.

Evaluation

Review your sketchbook and comment on its developing use.

Its main test is 'Does it give me all the information I need?'

Only by working from it will you know the answer to that.

Landscape stories

Claude Gellee (called Claude Lorrain) (1604–1682),
Landscape with David at the Cave of Adullam, 1658,
oil on canvas
112.4 × 185 cm (43 ⅝ × 72 ⅛ inches),
The National Gallery, London.

Sometimes landscapes have titles taken from the Bible or from Greek myths. The stories they tell had meaning for the person who commissioned the picture; the patron. They mean little to us, but we can still admire the beauty of the landscape the artist has given us.

Activity

Investigate other examples of works commissioned to illustrate stories from the Bible or Greek myths.

Claude Gellee (called Claude Lorrain) (1604–1682), **Landscape with Aenaeas at Delos**, 1672, oil on canvas, 99.7 × 134 cm (38 7/8 × 52 2/8 inches), The National Gallery, London.

Activity

Collect the resources that you need to create a landscape piece to illustrate a story like those shown here. You will need your sketchbook to make a study of trees, plants, figures, buildings and anything else you might require. Give your illustration a modern setting and a modern storyline. Set yourself targets before you begin, by writing a 'statement of intent'.

Evaluation

Make a display of the materials you have collected throughout your study. Show how they might be arranged in a final composition.

Can you explain your story?

Does the composition help?

Can other people interpret your story from your display?

Reading a landscape

David Ligare (b.1945),
Landscape for Baucis and Philemon, 1984,
oil on canvas,
81.3 × 122 cm (32 × 48 inches),
© Wadsworth Museum, Hartford Connecticut –
The Ella Gallup Sumner and Mary Catlin Sumner Collection Fund.

Activity

Cover up the caption of the picture above. Examine the picture and see how much information you can get from looking at the picture. You might, for example, be able to guess at the subject.

Uncover the caption and answer the questions:

1. Who painted this picture?
2. When was the artist alive, and when was this picture painted?
3. What is its title?
4. What materials were used to create it?
5. Where can it be seen today?
6. What is its size? (Remember height is always given first.)
7. Is the information given in the caption of value or can it be ignored?

Write your answers in full sentences.

The picture by Graham Ovenden recreates the atmosphere of early morning at a prehistoric tumulus. In the early morning light of the Downs it seems to have regained some of its ancient mystery.

Stone rings can often be found in Wiltshire. The open Downs were some of the first areas to be cleared of the forests that were once native to this area. The most famous of these stone circles is Stonehenge.

Graham Ovenden (b.1946),
Full moon over Silbury Hill, (1983),
oil on board, 30 × 24 cm (11 $^3/_4$ × 9 $^1/_4$ inches),
The Piccadilly Gallery, London.

Discussion point

★ Compare Constable's sketches on page 6 with the picture on this page. Which do you think catches the atmosphere best? How are they different?

Activity

Using the caption and information given in the text, write a paragraph describing Ovenden's painting in as much detail as possible.

Evaluation

Compare your descriptions with those of a friend.

Which of you has given the most comprehensive and informative description?

Talkback

Peter Paul Rubens (1577–1640),
Study of Trees, c. 17th century, pen and wash on paper,
58.1 × 48.6 cm (22¹¹⁄₁₆ × 18¹⁵⁄₁₆ inches),
Louvre, RMN Paris.

Discussion point

Look at the vocabulary in the word bank below.

★ Explain why these words have been included.
Use a dictionary to help you with any words you find difficult.

Word bank

horizon   background   balance   texture   depth
foreground   detail   form   perspective   composition
atmosphere   line   aerial perspective   subject   colour   space
contrast   light   time

Activity

Choose one of the pieces of work in this book. Use some of the words in the word bank to help you write about it.

Use the caption under the picture to help you. You might also find it helpful to use the list of questions on page 10 as a guide.

Peter Paul Rubens (1577–1640),
An Autumn Landscape with a view of Het Steen in the Early Morning, (1636),
oil on oak, 131.2 × 229.2 cm (51 $\frac{1}{8}$ × 89 $\frac{3}{8}$ inches),
The National Gallery, London.

Computer option

Use information stored on a CD–ROM or research the artist Peter Paul Rubens using the Internet as a source. Print out all you can about Peter Paul Rubens from your research.

Read the print-outs carefully and edit them so that you have a selection of the most useful pieces of information.

These steps will help you:

1. Decide what you need to know.
2. Use a highlighter to pick out the information.
3. Rewrite the highlighted sentences and link the relevant sentences together.
4. Check through your work to make sure you understand what you have written.
5. Word-process and spellcheck your work.

Extension

Use the same plan to write about the work of another artist whose work you like. Make an illustrated presentation of your research. You could use the vocabulary available on the opposite page.

OR

Use the information you have found from your research and a study of one of the pictures from this unit to present a short essay about Peter Paul Rubens.

Using landscape details

English Court Mantua and Petticoat, 1744, Victoria & Albert Museum, London.

Activity

Examine some of the small details that help make up a landscape. Make a record of them in your sketchbook. Include things like small plants, flowers and insects. Collect real specimens, press flowers, feathers, anything relevant you find interesting. Make your record more permanent by taking photographs.

Make colour studies in the field or when you return to the studio.

See if your sketchbook work improves your finished work.

Can you produce evidence to support this?

Evaluation

Use your sketchbook studies to create a detailed piece of work. It could be a print, painting or a design for a fabric. Start your design by grouping some of the more interesting pieces into a simple frieze or strip across the front of the work.

The English court dress above has an intricate amount of decoration on it. Without a knowledge of the plants it would be impossible to embroider. Use your detailed studies carefully, setting yourself clear targets before you begin work on your final piece.

Giovanni Bellini
(active about 1459, died 1516),
The Doge Leonardo Loredan, 1501–4,
oil on wood,
61.6 × 45.1 cm (24 × 17 ⅝ inches),
The National Gallery, London.

Activity

Look at the detail in the painting by Bellini.

Can you find some other similar examples of rich clothing in Renaissance paintings?

Look in particular for examples of works by Flemish artists who specialised in painting fine clothing. Research and make a detailed study of patterns on clothing by Flemish artists.

Evaluation

Collect and present your work as study sheets. Find ways in which you can improve your final piece of work.

Most work in sketchbooks, especially when working outside, needs to be refined before you can use it in your final piece of work. You need to work on sketches in the studio. Drawings that are to be used in a three-dimensional piece need to be developed as a simple trial piece, a 'maquette', before they can be used. In the Mantua opposite, the original plant drawings have come from a pattern book but the embroiders will have made samples before starting on the finished piece.

Present your development as study sheets, discuss them with others, and see if you can identify areas where they could have been improved.

The Japanese Landscape tradition

Katsushika Hokusai (1760–1849),
A Fisherman Standing on a Rocky Promontory at Kajikazawa in Kai Provence, from the series 'Thirty six views of Mt. Fuji', c. 1830–1831, colour woodblock print, 25 × 37.1 cm (9¾ × 14½ inches), Christie's Images/Bridgeman Art Library, London.

The colour woodblock print

Making a woodblock print the Japanese way involved many skilled craftsmen. The artist made a drawing on a sheet of rice paper. This was then transferred onto a woodblock. Then craftsmen cut away the wood to leave only the lines to be printed black showing and a black line print was made. The artist then coloured the print by hand and gave the coloured print back to the cutters who cut a separate block for each colour used.

Each block was then printed onto the black line print one after the other. Often as many as fifteen blocks were cut.

The main difficulty was getting the cut blocks to align correctly and there were many failures in the attempt to produce the 300 or so prints that made up a full edition. These failures, often used to wrap china were the inspiration for much Impressionist painting when the china was unpacked in Paris. Many can be seen behind portraits painted by this group.

Katsushika Hokusai (c. 1760–1849),
View of Mt. Fuji from the painted scroll of 'Twelve Views of Mt. Fuji',
early 19th century, colour woodblock print,
45.5 × 447 cm (17¾ × 174 inches),
Chester Beatty Library, Dublin/Bridgeman Art Library, London.

Both of these works are parts of a series. This was almost certainly due to the commercial pressure on the two artists whose work was in such demand that creating work in series seemed to make good commercial sense. To create works that fit together in this way is a productive way to work.

Extension

These Japanese artists use large areas of flat colour in their work: this is inherent in the colour woodcut process. This method influenced European artists who worked in the same way, firstly making a simple drawing and then using flat areas of colour in their picture. Can you find examples of artists who worked in this way?

Activity

Use your sketchbook to gather and keep the information you need and complete the series of work of your own that records your journey from home to school.

The details and the approach to your work may be influenced by the idea of a journey so that each person's work will be very individual.

Evaluation

Write an article for an art publication to explain your series of work. If you include examples make sure that they are properly captioned. You might like to try and find examples of written newspaper criticisms to base your own work on.

Turner's travels

JMW Turner (1775–1851), **Frandumont and the Bridge over the Hoege at Marche de Theux**, c. 1839, gouache, pen–and–ink and watercolour on blue paper,
14.4 × 19.3 cm (5⅝ × 7½ inches),
Tate Gallery, London.

Turner made many journeys. He often made a record of his travels. His journeys were not just to collect subjects for his paintings or his prints, they were an adventure that he often recaptured when he translated his sketches into oil paintings. He often noted the time of day to be sure that he positioned the sun, his light source, correctly.

Turner visited the Castle of Frandumont only once – he found out about it when illustrating a book of poetry by Sir Walter Scott. Turner was fascinated by the dramatic shape of the castle. He drew it from every angle as he approached it on his river journey down the Mosel. He even climbed to its gateway high above the river and drew the designs above the gate.

Activity

Make a journey – perhaps simply across a landscape you know well – on holiday or over a longer period of time. Make a record of your journey. Support your work with photographs.

From your record create a piece of work with a contrasting technique, using textiles or clay for example.

Evaluation

Collect and display the work that makes a pictorial record of your journey. Give a short presentation about your work.

Mark the places you have recorded on a sketch map of the area.

18

JMW Turner (1775–1851), **The Pont du Chateau and the Bock, Luxembourg**. c. 1839, gouache, pen–and–ink and watercolour on blue paper, 14 × 19 cm (5½ × 7½ inches) Tate Gallery, London.

Watercolours

Watercolours are made with finely ground pigments mixed with a gum-based binder. Watercolour paint is thinned and mixed with water and is usually applied in a thin wash or transparent film. Stronger colours and tones are built up by adding layer upon layer until the right colour intensity is reached. Watercolours are available in dry cakes of colour, in tubes, or in bottles. Turner's palette, on which he mixed his own hand-made oil colours, can be seen in the Tate Gallery, London.

Watercolours are best painted on heavy, stable papers that do not absorb too much water. Paper can be stretched to make it more acceptable.

You might find it of interest to look for other English artists whose watercolour work is much admired.

Watercolour is known as a medium in which English artists excelled.

Activity

Investigate the work of the Norwich School of Painters – painters who worked at a particular time around Norwich and in the medium of watercolour.

OR

Investigate other journeys that Turner made, for example, to the Lake District.

Extension

The watercolour technique relies on darkening tones or colours by adding more and more layers to an area.

See if you can prove this technique to yourself by doing some carefully recorded experiments. Choose a colour and lay down a wash. Cover half your area with a second coat when the first is dried. Cover half the area that has a second coat with a third coat and so on. Keep these experiments in your sketchbook.

Figures in landscape

David Inshaw (b. 1947), **The Badminton Game**, 1972–3, oil on canvas, 152 × 184 cm (59⁵⁄₁₆ × 71⅝ inches), Tate Gallery, London.

David Inshaw gives us the feeling that we have stumbled upon this friendly game in someone's garden. It is late on a hot sunny afternoon. Nothing seems out of place, the simplicity of the background draws our attention to the figures of the game.

Activity

Through working in your sketchbooks – both outside with real landscapes and from your imagination – create a simple landscape as a background to a figure or some figures. You can use some ready-made 3D figures or cut some from a magazine to fit into your designed landscape. Perhaps the figures could be deliberately chosen to look out of place.

Evaluation

Write a short description of your landscape piece.

Explain the story behind your figures in the landscape.

Do you think your choice of figures and the way they have been positioned has been effective?

Thomas Gainsborough (1727–1788), **Mr and Mrs Andrews**, c. 1748, oil on canvas, 70 × 199 cm (27⅝ × 46⅜ inches), The National Gallery, London.

Thomas Gainsborough painted this as a marriage portrait. The two sitters invite us to share the pride they have in the ownership of this fertile landscape.

Discussion points

Look at Thomas Gainsborough's image of the countryside.

★ Do you like his image and the way he has portrayed his characters in the landscape?

★ How does it compare with Inshaw's painting? How does it contrast with other images of landscape in this book?

Extension

Make a collection of landscapes used on decorating or wrapping paper, or as a part of an advertising image or found on labels. Keep the examples you have found and include them in your sketchbook.

★ How important are landscapes as part of the advertiser's creation of an image?

★ How realistic are these landscapes?

★ Are there some that create an image of old fashioned countryside and its people? Why do you suppose customers respond to products that look back to a landscape and the life of the past?

Write a paragraph on the use of landscapes in advertising to support your collection of examples.

Rural peace

Grant Wood (1891–1942), **Stone City, Iowa**, (1930),
oil on wood panel,
76.2 × 101.6 cm (30 × 40 inches),
Joslyn Art Museum, Omaha USA.

Grant Wood painted a series of pictures of the American Midwest. These were images of neat, well-organised landscapes without the disrupting influence of cars and roads and other twentieth century intrusions.

Stone City has the look of a child's toy rather than a real place. It is empty and silent.

Look at the way Wood has painted the trees and plants.

Discussion points

★ Are your landscapes based on imagination or observation?

★ Could you invent plants for your perfect landscape?

Activity

Create a perfect landscape of your own, the sort of place you might dream of living in. It might be a place of peace where even the plants live in neat ordered rows like the ones in Grant Wood's landscape. Use your sketchbook to develop your ideas. Set yourself a 'statement of intent' (see page 3) to help you. Remember, often your first ideas can be improved on.

Extension

This American artist painted one of the most famous paintings of the 20th century. It is called American Gothic.

Find out as much as you can about this work. What do you think of it?

Steve Easby (b. 1958), **In Daisy's Field**, 1991, acrylic on board, 76.2 × 76.2 cm (30 × 30 inches), Portal Gallery, London.

Steve Easby has painted a rural haven just as fanciful in its own way as the work of Grant Wood. The Horse Chestnut trees in flower are as inventive as the ordered, planted trees of *Stone City*. This vision of landscape as a place of peace and solitude is one which has appealed to artists for many years.

Discussion point

Do you think this romantic view of the countryside is real?

Activity

Use the vocabulary in the word bank below to help you describe the painting of Stone City by Grant Wood.

Alternatively, write a description of a garden or landscape you know well, using a selection of these words.

Word bank

tranquil peaceful solitude empty ordered tidy
gardens landscape fertile luscious regimented neat
clean weeded trimmed planted

Evaluation

Present your finished work as part of a group exhibition. The creation and delivery of posters and tickets need to be organised, as does the provision of refreshments. Divide up the tasks between the members of your group, then enjoy the public's evaluation of your work.

Looking for landscapes

Have you ever wondered what the world looked like before the age of the camera and television? Most of the evidence we have is from the works of artists. Artists who lived in the Netherlands were great masters of ordinary, every-day landscapes. Looking through the windows in their pictures gives us a true view of what their world was like. Robert Campin was one of these artists who under his own name (and the titles 'Master of Flamalle' and 'Master of Merode') is credited with the idea of painting townscapes and landscapes viewed through open windows in the background of his pictures.

Robert Campin (1378/9–1444)
The Virgin and Child before a firescreen,
c. 1440, oil on oak,
63.5 × 49.5 cm (24⅞ × 17⅝ inches),
The National Gallery, London.

Activity

Go on a journey through early fifteenth century Netherlands by looking through the windows of the paintings of the period. Artists from Venice also enjoyed painting real places into their pictures.

Collect your impression of either Venice or the Netherlands as sketches. Keep the evidence you have found in your sketchbook.

Create a piece depicting a background landscape suitable for a modern portrait. Concentrate on the background, the portrait could remain as a silhouette or a drawn round shadow.

Draw up a 'statement of intent' to show how you are going to approach this project. (See page 3.)

Jan van Eyck (c. 1390–1441), **The Virgin Chancellor Rollin**, c. 1435, oil on wood, panel, 66 × 62 cm (25⅝ × 24³⁄₁₆ inches), Louvre, RMN, Paris.

Extension

Complete the portrait as well as the background. You might then be able to explain why you have placed your sitter in the background you have designed for them.

Evaluation

Does the background in your portrait add to your understanding of the sitter?

Look back at your art historical studies. Can you identify the part played by these very accurate landscapes in our understanding of the artist's intentions?

Viewpoints

Andrew Wyeth (b. 1917), **Soaring**, 1950, tempera on masonite, 130 × 221 cm (50⅝ × 86⅗ inches), ©Shelburne Museum, Shelburne, Vermont.

We usually look at the landscape from a fixed viewpoint. Our eyes are set from between 4½ feet and 5½ feet from the ground—they look forward and parallel to the ground.

In a tall building or from an aircraft we look down, when climbing a steep road or stairs we look up, but in our normal day-to-day lives we have fixed vision.

Artists can fix our vision in any way they choose. They can freeze our vision from any viewpoint, however odd, and through their imagination hold it there. Next time you are watching a good quality film or animation, look for the drama that a change of viewpoint can create.

Wyeth liked unusual viewpoints, they are common in his work. Look at his work above—we are given the opportunity to soar with the vultures. They seem to be flying down to the little house in the empty landscape. A high viewpoint gives the artist more scope to include more landscape, a low viewpoint more clouds and sky.

Activity

Choose a place that you know well. From evidence collected on site and in your imagination, create a series of views from unusual angles. To help with your research create a plan or map. You could also collect illustrations from magazines or books that use unusual viewpoints. Experiment with high and low viewpoints.

Can you find other examples of Wyeth's work?

Bernard Carter (b. 1942), **Pelicans and Balloons at Leeds Castle**, (1979) oil on board, 27.9 × 40.6 cm (11 × 6 inches), Portal Gallery/Bridgeman Art Library, London.

Bernard Carter's work leads us into the picture before we look up at the balloons.

Evaluation

Place all your work together and pass it on to a friend. See if, from the evidence you have given, they can create a viewpoint different from yours.

Extension

Look at the illustrations in this book—you will see there is a wide variety.

Choose one of the illustrations that you really like and write a short paragraph about it.

Reference your writing with the full caption of your chosen illustration, so that others easily see which picture you are writing about.

Use the following three questions to help you plan your writing:

- Why have you chosen this piece?
- What is the piece of work about?
- What has the artist done to explain his intention? (An artist's intentions are not always easy to understand. Sometimes you have to look into the artist's own life and times to make sense of a piece of work. This is known as its context.)

Panoramas

Artists have always been asked to show views or illustrate places that are unknown. An example is on page 5 where the artist has created an aerial view long before it was possible to fly.

In 1787 a method to show towns and landscapes in a circular form was patented. The pictures were designed to give the viewer a more complete impression of a town or landscape. The artist, Robert Barker, created a number of landscapes by turning on the spot through 360 degrees while drawing all the major landmarks and features, thus capturing a full panoramic view. He always chose locations that gave impressive views of the surroundings.

Ramsay R Reiunagle, Panorama of Florence (1812),

The idea caught on and soon there were many of these views printed on cloth and paper. The viewer could recognise the most noticeable features and understand the relationships between them by simply turning the drawing around. Eventually these elaborate drawings were placed in specially built circular rooms and people visited them much as they might visit a cinema today.

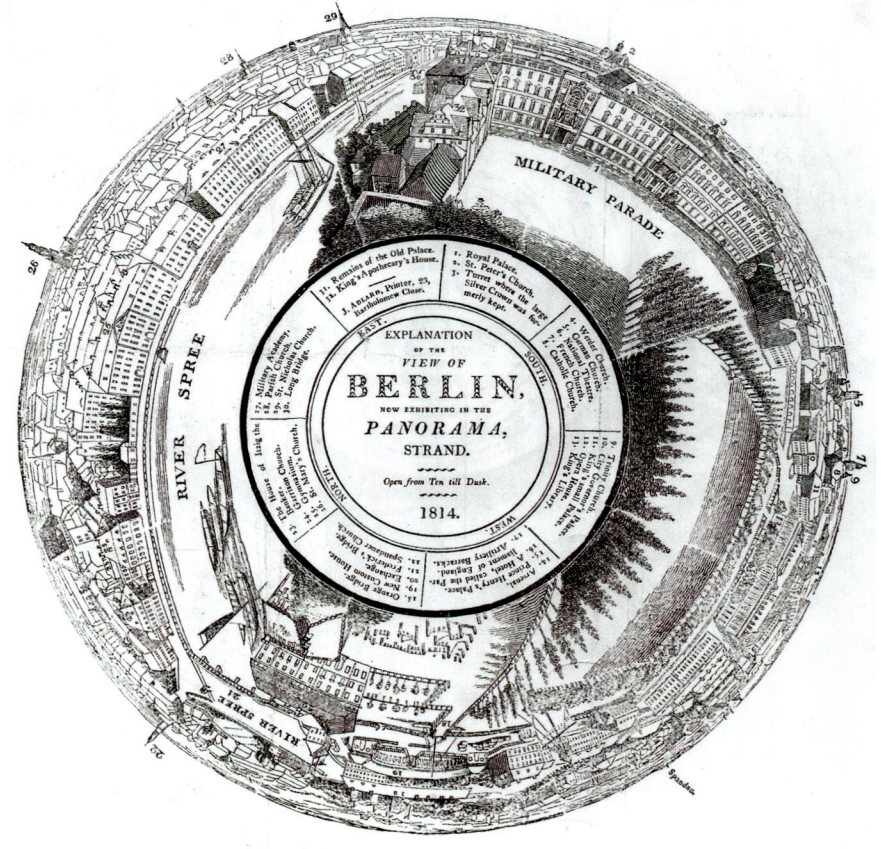

Ramsay R Reiunagle,
Panorama of Berlin (1814),
engravings from an illustrated pamphlet, British Library, London.

New York photographed through fish-eye lens, photographed by Charles & Rotkin

Activity

Choose a spot near your home or school from which you would get a good view of the surrounding area, and on a large sheet of paper draw a circle. Imagine you are in the centre of the circle and, working logically, draw the builidngs or other landmarks that you might see. Work your way round until you have completed the circle.

Evaluation

Share your completed drawing with others from your class who know the area you have chosen well. Compare your ideas of where these landmarks might be. You might like to take advice and, if you feel the need to, correct your drawing accordingly.

Extension

A fish-eye lens, like in the photograph above, will show a 360 degree hemisphere of your surroundings. You can create a similar but narrower view by taking successive photographs as you turn through 360 degrees (just like Barker did). This panorama will provide you with a complete circular view. It will be an invaluable aid if you review your drawing.

New landscapes

This piece of work by Andy Goldsworthy will have had a short life. It shows how an artist can work with the landscape rather than just make a record of it. By selecting and grading different colours of maple leaves in autumn, he created a piece that added to the landscape itself.

Andy Goldsworthy (b. 1956), **Line to explore colours in leaves, calm, overcast**, Ouchiyama-mura Japan, 14 November 1987, photograph, reproduced courtesy of the artist.

Activity

Working out of doors with only natural materials, create a piece of sculpture that adds to the landscape it stands in. Consider the landscape that you will be working in and be prepared to collect raw materials from it. Keep a photographic record of your work.

For this activity organise yourselves to work in a group. Create a 'statement of intent' before you begin (see page 3).

Evaluation

Invite visitors to your site to write their comments, either in a site book or directly into your sketchbook. Visitors could be encouraged to visit while your work is being constructed and even have some input into the final product through their suggestions.

Richard Long (b. 1945), **Mountain Lake**, Powder Snow, Lapland, 1985, photograph courtesy of Anthony d'Offay Gallery, London.

Look at the work by the artist Richard Long – you will not be able to work on this scale! This is an aerial photograph of his work. Though his work will have not survived long, except as a photograph, it can still be considered a reformation of the landscape.

Compare this with the work of South American civilisations that marked the high desert landscapes of the Andes with the figures of birds and other animals. Their art could only have been recognised from the air.

Can you imagine what Richard Long's circle would look like from ground level?

Extension

Find out all you can about other artists that work to the same scale as Richard Long's landscape work. Write a short definition of the idea of 'Land Art' and choose an illustration from amongst the work you have researched that you think expresses that definition best. The following may give you some good starting points:

- *The South American civilisations of the Andes*
- *Capability Brown – the 18th century landscape designer*
- *Cristo who set up hundreds of yellow and blue umbrellas over the landscape.*

For Dianne, Serena, Beech and Sapphire

Acknowledgements

The publishers would like to thank the following individuals, institutions and companies for permission to reproduce photographs in this book. Every effort has been made to trace ownership of copyright. The publishers will be happy to make arrangements with any copyright holder whom it has not been possible to contact.

Andy Goldsworthy 30; Anthony d'Offay Gallery, London 31; British Library 28 (top and bottom); British Museum, London 5; Charles & Rotkin 29; Chester Beatty Library/Bridgeman Art Library 17; Christie's Images/Bridgeman Art Library 16; Courtauld Institute of Art, London 6 (bottom);Frick Collection, New York 4;Joslyn Art Museum, Omaha 22; Louvre, RMN, Paris 12, 25; The National Gallery, London 2, 8, 9, 13, 15, 21, 24; The Piccadilly Gallery, London 11; Portal Gallery, London 3, 23; Portal Gallery/ Bridgeman Art Library 27; Shelburne Museum, Vermont 26; Tate Gallery, London 18, 19, 20; Victoria & Albert Museum 6 (top), 7, 14; Wandsworth Museum, Hartford, Connecticut 10;

Orders: please contact Bookpoint Ltd, 78 Milton Park, Abingdon, Oxon OX14 4TD. Telephone: (44) 01235 827720, Fax: (44) 01235 400454. Lines are open from 9.00 - 6.00, Monday to Saturday, with a 24 hour message answering service. Email address: orders@bookpoint.co.uk

British Library Cataloguing in Publication Data
A catalogue record for this title is available from The British Library

ISBN 0 340 66415 0

First published 2000
Impression number 10 9 8 7 6 5 4 3 2 1
Year   2005 2004 2003 2002 2001 2000

Copyright © 2000 Chris Dunn

All rights reserved. No part of this publication may be reproduced or transmitted in any form or by any means, electronic or mechanical, including photocopy, recording, or any information storage and retrieval system, without permission in writing from the publisher or under licence from the Copyright Licensing Agency Limited. Further details of such licences (for reprographic reproduction) may be obtained from the Copyright Licensing Agency Limited, of 90 Tottenham Court Road, London W1P 9HE.

Cover photo: Grant Wood, **Stone City**, **Iowa**, oil on wood panel, ($30\frac{1}{4}$ x 40 inches), Joslyn Art Museum, Omaha, USA
Designed by Lynda King
Typeset by Ian Foulis & Associates, Plymouth, Devon
Picture research by Suzanne O'Farrell
Printed in Dubai, U.A.E. for Hodder & Stoughton Educational, a division of Hodder Headline Plc, 338 Euston Road, London NW1 3BH by Oriental Press